C000054782

Depression

*How to Cure Depression
Naturally Without
Resorting to Harmful
Meds*

Robert S. Lee

Contents

Introduction

Major depression affects approximately 19 million adults in the United States. The majority of these people will be prescribed powerful antidepressant medications to try and control their symptoms. However, depression is an illness and just controlling the symptoms does not help someone to fully recover. It is important to treat the symptoms at their core and uncover the cause of depression to ensure recovery.

Depression causes a number of serious symptoms, both emotional and physical. The most common depression symptoms include:

- Feeling empty, sad and unhappy

- Loss of interest

- Lack of energy and fatigue

- Agitation, anxiety and restlessness

- Feeling guilty or worthlessness

- Thoughts of death

- Irritability, anger or frustration

- Sleeping problems

- Appetite changes

- Slowed thinking, body movements and speaking

- Difficulty with decision making, memory, concentration and thinking

- Unexplainable physical symptoms, such as digestive complaints, headaches and back pain

Masking these symptoms can make you feel better, but it does not take care of the problem so that they are permanently relieved. There are natural depression treatments that set out to treat the total mind and body. These help to address the root of your depression while also alleviating your symptoms. This allows for a higher level of productivity and an improved mood and you recover from depression. You can combine a mixture of natural remedies to enhance your symptom relief and reduce the time that it takes you to recover from depression.

Chapter 1. Create a Routine and Reasonable Goals

Depression can make your world chaotic and it can make it difficult to tackle all of your daily responsibilities. It is important to take control and create a routine and set reasonable goals. These two factors give you something to work toward on a daily basis so that you do not feel like you are lost. Start with creating a routine so that you have a basis for creating and pursuing your goals. The following tips will help you to start a routine that works for you so that you can start getting back to normal and feeling better:

- **Ease into your routine:** Instead of making abrupt changes, make small changes that add up to a bigger change down the line. For example, make it a point to put the dishes in the dishwasher after dinner each day. This small change will help you to normalize your daily routine.

- **Write it down:** Some people find is easier to follow a routine when they have it in front of them. Just make sure to give yourself adequate time for each task.

- **Detail your schedule:** Assign a start and end time to each task.

- **Create a checklist:** If some of your tasks are made up of multiple tasks, create checklists for them. This will prevent you from forgetting to do something important.

- **Make adjustments:** If your routine is not working for you, look at it and make some adjustments. You can change it daily, weekly or any time that you feel it is not helping you.

- **Know your rhythm:** Some people feel better during certain times of the day. For example, some people experience more symptoms of depression after sundown. If this is you, you would center your routine around daylight hours as much as possible.

- **Ask for help:** If some of your tasks are too much for you, ask someone to help you out.

When you have a good routine, you will work to reduce symptoms like memory problems, difficulty making decisions and concentration problems. Your routine essentially gives you a roadmap that you can follow each day to ensure that you address all of your responsibilities.

Creating goals is important because it gives you something positive to look forward to. Having goals helps you to prevent your depression from taking full control of your life. When you are setting goals, make sure that they are reasonable because setting overly ambitious goals that you cannot accomplish can actually worsen your depression. Use the following guidelines to establish reasonable goals and help yourself stick to them:

- Be positive with your goals and write them down in a positive manner

- Set your priorities for each goal to ensure timely completion

- Break your big goals into small goals so that nothing becomes overwhelming

- Keep your eye on the big picture

- Be precise when you are constructing your goals

- Give yourself an adequate start and end date for your goals

- Write your goals down somewhere that allows you to see them each morning

- Be flexible and make alterations when necessary to complete your goals

Chapter 2. Physical Activity

Studies going back decades show that getting regular physical activity provides both a short-term and long-term boost in mood. It is not completely clear exactly why regular physical activity benefits depression, but experts believe that it is associated with the following:

- Exercise releases brain chemicals that naturally elevate your mood

- Exercise provides a calming effect due to increasing your body temperature

- Certain chemicals in the immune system can make depression worse and exercises reduces these chemicals

In addition to the biological benefits for depression, physical activity can also benefit depression in the following ways:

- **Increased confidence:** Those who exercise regularly and meet their fitness goals earn a boost in confidence. It can also improve how you feel about your appearance. Confidence can help to reduce the severity of depression symptoms.

- **More social interaction:** Many people with depression isolate themselves, but this just furthers your depressive symptoms. Join an exercise class, head to the gym or get your physical activity with a friend to increase your social interaction.

- **Distracting you from worry:** When you are depressed, it is natural to worry about the things that are out of your control and this feeds into negative thoughts that deepen your depression. When you are getting physical activity, this helps to release those mood-boosting brain chemicals that make you feel better and not think about your worries.

- **Healthy way of coping:** Physical activity gives you a positive way to deal with your depression. For example, when you are feeling down, taking a walk can boost your mood and help you to cope.

Several studies show that the positive mood-boosting effects of exercise last longer than the mood-boosting effects of antidepressants. One study in the *Archives of Internal Medicine* published in 1999 looked at how exercise affected 156 patients. One group was prescribed the SSRI medication Zoloft, one group only exercised and a third group did both exercise and take Zoloft.

The results of this study after 16 weeks show that all groups had an improvement in their depression. However, researchers followed up with 133 patients from this study after six months. This showed that the patients who continued to only get physical activity maintained their results and were far less likely to relapse and experience another bout of depression. This shows that regular physical activity is more powerful and more effective than antidepressant medications. Physical activity is more likely to promote recovery and prevent relapse compared to antidepressant medications.

Many people are turned off by the thought of regular exercise. It is important to stay focused on the term "physical activity" because this means a lot more than exercise. The key is to get moving in a way that you find fun so that you will continue do it. You can choose to take walks, play with your pets or children, go for a swim or play a sport. These will all give you the same benefits as exercise without the tedious repetition. You want to strive for 30 minutes each day and you can choose a different physical activity each day.

Just make sure that the activity that you choose increases your heart rate and has you moving for the majority of the time. For example, if you enjoy shooting a basketball, also make sure to retrieve your own rebounds to keep moving as you shoot around.

If you do enjoy regular exercise, the same guidelines apply that you want to get 30 minutes a day. Strive for cardiovascular exercise at least five days a week. Exercise like running, walking at a moderate pace, swimming, cycling and using cardio machines at the gym are all good forms of cardiovascular exercise.

You do not have to do the full 30 minutes in one stint. If it is easier, break up this time into three 10-minute physical activity or exercise sessions. You can also add additional physical activity to your day by doing the following:

- Walk more by parking further from the store

- Take a walk on your lunch break

- Skip the elevator and take the stairs

- Walk to work if you live close

- Walk your dog instead of just letting him or her outside

Getting started with physical activity is the hardest part, but once you do get started, you will find that it is something that is easy to maintain. Use the following steps to start your physical activity regimen:

- **Identify the activities that you enjoy:** It is important that you focus on the types of physical activity that you like because this will help you to stick with what you are doing.

- **Set reasonable goals:** Goals are critical for those with depression, but the goals must be reasonable to be helpful. Start small and work your way up, especially if you are not already active. For example, start off with 10 minutes of an activity that you enjoy each day. Every week, add an additional five minutes to this activity until you reach 30 minutes a day.

- **Analyze your barriers:** Depression presents a set of barriers that often leads to people not putting emphasis on physical activity and other healthy things. It is important that you take the time to learn what your barriers are so that you can confront and overcome them.

- **Be prepared for setbacks:** There will be times when you skip a day or do not get your full time in. Be prepared for these so that they do not further affect your mood. You simply need to get back to your physical activity schedule the next day and not dwell on the days that you missed.

Chapter 3. Diet and Foods

Your diet plays a role in all aspects of your health and this includes your mental health. There are many foods that can actually help you to feel better as you recover from depression. On the other hand, certain foods may actually play into your depression symptoms and make them worse.

Experts believe that many nutritional factors may contribute to depression and its symptoms. For example, certain nutrient deficiencies of imbalances may contribute to someone developing depression, such as:

- Someone does not get enough Omega-3 fatty acids

- People not getting enough amino acids, resulting in a reduction in serotonin

- A person may have food intolerances feeding into their depression symptoms

- Their blood sugar is not in balance, making mood symptoms worse

- Levels of homocysteine in the body are too high

- Low levels of vitamin D and chromium in the body

Starting with these factors, there are many things that you can start doing to alleviate your depression via your diet. Omega-3 fatty acids are a nutrient that the body does not create on its own, so you must get it through your diet. The best way to get more of this nutrient in your diet is by eating a variety of fish, such as salmon, mackerel, herring, fresh tuna, sardines and trout. Countries with a low incidence of omega-3 fatty acid deficiency also tend to have a very low incidence of depression. Evidence suggests that the EPA that omega-3 fatty acids contain work as a powerful natural antidepressant.

B vitamins play a critical role in your mood and the B vitamin folic acid actually has similar effects to SSRI antidepressants without the side effects. In fact, those who get plenty of folic acid, vitamin B6 and vitamin B12 are significantly less likely to develop depression. You can get more B vitamins in your diet by eating plenty of fortified foods, fish, lean meats, low-fat dairy, poultry and eggs.

You need to get plenty of amino acids, especially tryptophan, because this works to ensure adequate levels of serotonin in the body. Tryptophan is turned into 5-hydroxy tryptophan, another amino acid in the body. This is then turned into serotonin, a brain chemical known as a neurotransmitter that plays a critical role in mood stabilization. Get more tryptophan in your diet by eating plenty of fresh fish, eggs, lean meats and beans.

Your blood sugar levels have a major impact on your mood. Whether your levels are too high or too low, this can cause you to experience things like irritability and inability to focus or concentrate. Avoid foods that cause a spike and crash, such as sugar and simple carbohydrates (white bread and white rice are common examples). Stick to whole grains because these contain complex carbohydrates which give you sustained blood sugar levels.

Chromium is a type of mineral that plays a major role in blood sugar stabilization. Insulin requires this mineral to work properly and keep your blood sugar levels stables. Research shows that people with adequate chromium levels are less likely to experience depression or mood-related problems. You can get more chromium in your diet by eating more high-bran cereals, green beans, nuts, whole grains, egg yolk and broccoli.

You also need to ensure adequate vitamin D levels because research is showing that vitamin D deficiency may be linked to depression and mood issues. This is especially true for those who experience depressive symptoms during the winter months when there is less daylight each day. The best way to get vitamin D is naturally via exposure to sunlight. However, you can also eat fortified foods or take a high-quality supplement.

There are certain foods that can help to boost your mood, both short-term and long-term. When you eat these foods, you notice a boost in your mood almost immediately. When you eat these foods on a regular basis, you will notice that your mood is better overall. Incorporate the following foods into your diet to alleviate your depression symptoms:

- **Turkey:** Turkey contains tryptophan which increases serotonin levels for a better mood.

- **Walnuts:** This food contains mood-boosting omega-3 fatty acids.

- **Salmon:** Salmon and other fatty fish alleviate depression due to containing omega-3 fatty acids.

- **Low-fat dairy:** Adequate vitamin D levels are critical for fighting depression and low-fat dairy is a rich source of this vitamin.

- **Whole grains:** Whole grains work to stabilize your blood sugar which helps to improve your mood.

- **Green tea:** Green tea is a superfood because it offers over two dozen health benefits. The theanine present in this type of tea helps to promote a relaxed alertness.

- **Turmeric:** Turmeric is a popular spice that helps to improve your mood and reduce inflammation thanks to the compounds curcuminods and turmerones.

- **Dark chocolate:** Dark chocolate is another superfood that boosts your mood by promoting the release of serotonin in the body.

- **Asparagus:** Asparagus contains a high level of folic acid, a vitamin critical for a balanced mood.

- **Avocado:** This popular vegetable is rich in folic acid, as well as vitamin E, lutein and beta-carotene. These nutrients play a role in helping you to manage your stress.

- **Blueberries:** This superfood helps to improve cognition and focus thanks to anthocyanin, a powerful antioxidant.

- **Oatmeal:** Having a bowl of oatmeal in the morning is a great way to start off your day in a great mood because it helps to encourage serotonin production.

In addition to the information above that works to alleviate your depression, you also want to know about foods that may actually have a negative effect on your mood. To improve and maintain a better mood, avoid the following foods as much as possible:

- **Agave nectar:** This food can cause mood instability by acutely increasing blood sugar levels. Consider 100 percent organic maple syrup as a better alternative.

- **Conventional ham:** These foods are packed with nitrates and these can promote a poor mood. Switch to a wild caught salmon instead for a burst of mood-boosting omega-3 fatty acids.

- **Soda:** You already know that soda is unhealthy, but it directly affects your mood by causing your blood sugar to spike and plummet. Consider soda water instead if you want a fizzy drink.

- **Margarine:** Margarine is packed with omega-6 fatty acids and in excess, these tamper with insulin levels and negatively affect your mood. Choose a pastured butter instead to get a boost of omega-3 fatty acids.

- **Processed pumpkin seeds:** This food can cause a poor mood by affecting your thyroid. Choose raw pumpkin seeds instead for a burst of important trace minerals.

- **Potato chips:** Potato chips are also high in omega-6 fatty acids which block out omega-3 fatty acids. Consider microwavable popcorn instead when you want a crunchy snack.

- **Bagels:** Bagels are packed with simple carbohydrates, causing a surge of energy and a major crash a couple of hours later, worsening depression-related fatigue.

Opt for organic eggs instead for sustained energy.

- **Peanuts:** Processed peanuts are packed with food additives that may worsen your mood and promote headaches. Choose healthier nuts, such as almonds and walnuts for a dose of natural antidepressant nutrients, such as selenium.

Research shows that gluten may also cause depressive symptoms if someone has a gluten sensitivity, intolerance or Celiac disease. In addition to depression, other signs of gluten issues include digestive issues shortly after eating, such as constipation, diarrhea and upset stomach. Unexplained anemia can also indicate a problem with gluten.

Chapter 4. Lifestyle Changes to Improve Sleep

Sleep and depression play into one another because poor sleep can increase depression symptoms and depression can cause poor sleep. Because of this strong link, it is important to take the steps necessary to get the best sleep possible each night. There are many lifestyle changes and habit changes that you can start making today to improve both the quality and length of your sleep each night. You will notice an improvement in your mood almost immediately when you start sleeping better.

Limit Your Bedroom Activities

When you are preparing to go to sleep, there are many activities that can keep you awake and you want these out of your bedroom. Experts often say that your bedroom should only serve two purposes and these include sex and sleeping. Everything else needs to stay out of your bedroom since they can distract you from sleep. Move the television out, leave your laptop in your office and keep your hobbies out of your bedroom. The point is to make your bedroom a place that relaxes you and only allows for relaxation.

Enjoy a Light Late Night Snack

A bedtime snack that is light and contains certain nutrients can help to induce sleep. The key is to choose a snack that has nutrients that will promote more serotonin and melatonin, two natural substances in the body that promote sleep. Look for foods that contain the amino acid tryptophan because this will have this effect. Your snack should be under 200 calories and it should not be filling. You just want something light that satisfies you. The following foods contain high amounts of sleep-promoting tryptophan:

- Squash and pumpkin seeds

- Soy-based foods

- Cheese

- Turkey

- Chicken

- Fish and shellfish

- Oats and oat bran

- Lentils and beans

- Whole eggs

You can eat these foods in any combination, depending on your preferences. You can also add other healthy foods. Just make sure to avoid anything that can interfere with your sleep, such as sugars, simple carbohydrates and caffeine.

Create and Stick to a Sleep Schedule

You want to start your pre-bed routine and go to bed at the same time every night. It is also important to set your alarm for the same time every morning. Ideally, there will be no more than an hour difference between the days when you wake up and go to sleep. When you have a sleep schedule, your circadian rhythm – which is your body's internal clock – adjusts and makes it easier to fall asleep, stay asleep and wake up.

It can take time to get into a good schedule and sleep through the night so make sure to practice patience. The key is to be actively working toward a regular sleep schedule and your body will recognize that you are training it.

Stop Consuming Caffeine at Noon

Caffeine is one of the most popular ways to boost and maintain your energy throughout the day because it stimulates your central nervous system. However, this means that your nervous system is still stimulated when you are trying to sleep at night, preventing sleep. Having a cup or two of coffee in the morning is fine and may actually be beneficial for those with depression. However, once noon rolls around, stop drinking coffee so that the caffeine does not interfere with your sleep.

If you truly enjoy coffee, you can switch to decaffeinated coffee after the noon hour. It is also important that you are mindful of other things that contain caffeine in addition to coffee.

The most common sources of caffeine after coffee include teas, chocolate and soda. Make sure to read labels well and choose teas and sodas that are free from caffeine. There are many teas that come without caffeine, giving you a variety of options. When it comes to chocolate, there is no such thing as a caffeine-free chocolate, so you want to refrain from eating chocolate, especially dark chocolate, close to your bedtime.

Skip Taking Naps

Depression makes you tired and is zaps your energy, so it seems like taking a nap may be beneficial, but it will actually have a negative impact on your sleep. It is important to skip those naps and find other ways to boost your energy when you are feeling tired during the day. Even an hour nap can make it harder to fall asleep and stay asleep at night. Consider taking a walk, stretching or eating something with complex carbohydrates for a boost of energy during the day because none of these will prevent you from getting restful sleep.

Breathe Deeply Before Bed

Deep breathing is incredibly relaxing and it helps to calm you. Many people feel anxious before bed and this is an easy way to combat this. Start by getting comfortable, either sitting or lying down on your bed. Close your eyes and push the negative thoughts from your mind so that you can clear your mind. Breathe in for 10 seconds, inhaling slowly and focusing on your belly getting sucked in. Hold this breath in for 10 seconds and then slowly exhale over 10 seconds. As you exhale, you want to imagine all of the negatives leaving your body.

Deep breathing is a way to cleanse yourself of everything negative that may have affected you that day. This will calm your mind and body so that you are able to sleep peacefully and start the next morning without negative influences. All of those thoughts that usually keep you awake are now gone and you can focus on quieting your mind so that you ease into a deep and restful sleep. You should take five to ten breaths to cleanse your mind and body and allow for total relaxation. Do not rush through this and make sure to follow the 10-second rule for every breath.

Start and Stick to a Relaxing Pre-Bed Routine

A relaxing bedtime routine is critical for falling asleep quickly and staying asleep. About 30 minutes before your established bedtime, you want to start this routine so that it has time to relax you. Start by turning off all televisions, computers and your cellphone. You want to avoid looking at the screens on these devices because the light that they emit can keep you awake.

Next, choose an activity that helps you to feel calm and relaxed. Things like reading or listening to relaxing music are common options.

Some people also like to stretch gently or simply lie back and reflect on the positive aspects of their day. The key is to find something that relaxes you and do this every night.

Consider a Cup of Tea Before Bed

There are several types of tea that are known for promoting relaxation. Enjoying a cup as you go through your relaxing pre-bed routine can help you to ease into sleep and sleep better throughout the night. There are several teas that you can consider, including:

- Chamomile tea

- St. John's Wort tea

- Catnip tea

- Valerian tea

- Lemon balm tea

- Peppermint tea

- Green tea

- Lavender tea

- Passion flower tea

- Kava tea

- Ashwaganda tea

- California poppy tea

- Rhodiola rosea root tea

- Skullcap tea

Exercise Every Day

You learned in a previous chapter how beneficial regular physical activity is for depression. One of the benefits is that regular exercise helps you to sleep. Try to avoid exercise right before bed because this can actually rev up your body and prevent sleep. However, when you exercise regularly in the morning or afternoon, this will help ease you into sleep each night.

You can start making all of these changes and improving your sleep today. You will start noticing the positive effects right away. If it is easier, start with one change and incorporate a new one each week until you are using all of them to get better sleep and ease your depression symptoms.

Make sure that you are consistent with your lifestyle and habit changes for sleep. It is important to make time for this because good sleep is critical for alleviating the symptoms of depression. Make schedule changes if necessary to make sleep a priority. You want to set aside about 30 minutes every night for your pre-bed routine and approximately eight hours for sleeping. Ideally, you will give yourself nine hours each day for your pre-bed routine and sleep so that you never feel rushed.

Chapter 5.
Supplements

There are many supplements that are known to be effective in working to fight against depression. These supplements help to ensure that your body has what it needs for a stable mood and optimal health. Before you start using any supplements for depression, make sure that you talk to your doctor. You want to ensure optimal safety and the right dosage so that you reap the full benefits of the supplements that you choose.

<u>B Vitamins</u>

Earlier in this book, you learned how critical the B vitamins are for your mood and fighting depression. It is critical that you get adequate amounts of all of the B vitamins each day to ensure a stable mood. You want to concentrate most on your intake of folic acid, vitamin B6 and vitamin B12. Use the following guidelines to ensure an adequate intake:

- **Vitamin B 12:** People ages 14 and older need 2.4 micrograms each day.

- **Vitamin B6:** People ages 19 to 50 need 1.3 milligrams each day. Men over age 50 need 1.7 milligrams each day and women over age 50 need 1.5 milligrams each day.

- **Folic acid:** People ages 19 and older need 400 micrograms each day.

Magnesium

Magnesium is necessary for multiple biochemical functions and producing energy. If you are depressed, this can deplete your magnesium levels, so supplementing can help to keep your levels in balance. When you are getting enough magnesium, this helps to counteract the fatigue and lack of energy that are common with depression. Magnesium also helps to stabilize blood sugar levels to prevent mood problems associated with high or low blood sugar. The following are the recommended intake amounts for this nutrient:

- **Women ages 19 to 30**: 310 milligrams

- **Women ages 31 to 50**: 320 milligrams

- **Women over age 51**: 320 milligrams

- **Men ages 19 to 30**: 400 milligrams

- **Men ages 31 to 50**: 420 milligrams

- **Men over age 51**: 420 milligrams

Vitamin D

There is a strong correlation between vitamin D deficiency and depression. Studies show that the lower a person's vitamin D levels are, the higher their risk of depression. Some research also indicates that depression may have a negative impact on vitamin D levels.

The following are the recommended daily intake amounts for vitamin D:

- **All adults ages 19 to 70**: 600 IU per day

- **All adults over age 70**: 800 IU per day

Chromium

Chromium is a trace mineral that is necessary for multiple body functions. It affects how sensitive the cells are to insulin to ensure that serotonin is able to travel across the blood-brain barrier. This means that without adequate chromium levels in the body, you may have low levels of serotonin and low serotonin results in a depressed mood and a much greater risk for developing depression. This trace mineral may also have a positive effect on other brain chemicals that are responsible for balancing and stabilizing your mood.

The following describe the recommended daily intakes for chromium:

- **Men ages 19 to 50:** 35 micrograms per day

- **Men over age 50:** 30 micrograms per day

- **Women ages 19 to 50:** 25 micrograms per day

- **Women over age 50:** 20 micrograms per day

SAM-e

SAM-e is produced in the body and it is necessary for neurotransmitter synthesis. Without adequate levels of this substance, you may have an imbalance of neurotransmitters which has a direct impact on your mood. Some studies conclude that SAM-e supplements may work similar to antidepressants in balancing chemicals in the brain that stabilize the mood. There are studies that state that a SAM-e supplement is at least as effective as certain prescription antidepressants. Supplements of

SAM-e provide you with a stabilized form of this substance which is naturally produced when adenosyl-triphosphate (ATP) and the amino acid methionine combine in the body.

Probiotics

The health of your gut has a significant impact on your mental health. In fact, your gut has nerve cells that are responsible for producing approximately 80 to 90 percent of the serotonin in the body. You need serotonin for a balanced and stabilized mood. Probiotics work to keep your digestive system working optimally so that the nerve cells located in your gut are able to work and produce serotonin without interruption.

Omega-3 Fatty Acids

Omega-3 fatty acids play a major role when it comes to your mood. The EPA component of omega-3 fatty acids balances omega-6 arachidonic acid levels to ensure mood stabilization. When you are looking for a supplement, the ideal range is a 7:1 ratio of EPA to DHA with 70 percent EPA.

Amino Acids

When you are not getting enough amino acids, you get sluggish, lose focus, feel foggy and are at risk for depression. Your body needs amino acids to create the neurotransmitters that stabilize and boost your mood. There are nine essential amino acids that you must get regularly, including:

- Histidine

- Leucine

- Methionine

- Threonine

- Valine

- Isoleucine

- Lysine

- Phenylalanine

- Tryptophan

<u>GABA</u>

You can find GABA in supplement form and studies show that these supplements may have a positive impact on depression symptoms. GABA is a type of neurotransmitter with anti-anxiety effects. In fact, the most common prescription anti-anxiety medications, such as Xanax, Ativan and Valium, relax and calm the nervous system by acting on GABA pathways.

Melatonin

Melatonin does not directly impact depression, but it is critical for regulating the sleep-wake cycle to reduce the insomnia that commonly occurs with depression. Good sleep is critical for improving mood and preventing the overwhelming lack of energy that depression can cause. Melatonin comes in many dosages and to ensure that you are getting the right dose, talk to your doctor and discuss the dosage together.

If you think that a nutrient deficiency of any of the nutrients discussed above could be playing a role in your depression, talk to your doctor. Blood testing can be done to see if you are suffering from any nutrient deficiencies. If there is a nutrient deficiency present, you may need to take a prescription supplement to help correct the deficiency and restore the deficient nutrient to optimal levels. Once your nutrient levels are back to where they need to be, you can take an over-the-counter supplement to prevent future nutrient deficiency problems.

Chapter 6. Herbs

Herbs are one of the most commonly used natural remedies to fight depression. There are a number of herbs that you can consider that work similar to prescription antidepressant medications. To ensure absolute safety, make sure that you talk to your doctor before using any herbs. Your doctor can also help you to take the right dose so that you reap the most benefits from the herbs that you choose to take.

St. John's Wort

St. John's Wort is probably the most popular herb used for depression. The use of this herb goes back to ancient Greece where physicians used it to alleviate the symptoms of mild or moderate depression. This herb contains a compound called hypercin which seems to have a positive effect on the neurotransmitters in the brain. In fact, it works similar to Prozac and other serotonin reuptake inhibitors, but with a much lower risk of unpleasant side effects. To use this herb, you will need to find a high-quality supplement and these most commonly come in capsule form.

You should have your dosage tailored to you, but the general dosage is 300 milligrams taken three times per day.

Nutmeg

Nutmeg may be used for both depression and anxiety. Studies done on animals show that this herb works similar to both antidepressant and anti-anxiety medications. It has a calming effect and it helps to relax you. This helps with depression overall, but also with some of the common symptoms, such as muscle tension and insomnia. To use nutmeg, you would use it in its powder form by adding one-eighth of a teaspoon to fresh juice. Drink this twice a day.

Saffron

Saffron is an herb that is works to increase feel-good brain chemicals, including serotonin. This is thanks to it containing healthy doses of B vitamins and carotenoids. Studies show that saffron has the ability to reduce mild to moderate depression at least as effectively as the prescription antidepressant Prozac. To use saffron, ingest 15 milligrams twice a day of the dried extract.

Lemon Balm

Lemon balm helps with depression in many ways by helping to relax and calm you, lift your spirits, ease insomnia and alleviate tension. The average dose of this herb is 600 milligrams once per day. You can also create a tea using fresh lemon balm leaves. Take two to three teaspoons of the leaves and steep them in boiling water for about 20 minutes. You can drink this tea up to three times daily.

Green Tea

Green tea is popular for depression because it works to boost your mood throughout the day with a single cup. It contains caffeine and L-theanine. The two work together to boost your mood and your energy without causing a crash later in the day. It crosses the blood-brain barrier, providing psychoactive properties to help boost GABA, a brain inhibitory transmitter and dopamine, a neurotransmitter. Both of these work to improve your mood.

Since green tea contains caffeine, you want to have a cup of it early in the morning and avoid this later in the day so that it does not disrupt your sleep. Simply steep a green tea bag in a cup of boiling water and drink it. You can add some honey or fresh lemon for taste.

Skullcap

Skullcap works to strengthen the nervous system and calm you. This helps with several depression symptoms, such as difficulty concentrating, poor sleep and headaches. One benefit to this herb is that there are several ways to take it, making it convenient. You can make a tea by steeping a teaspoon of the dried herb in a cup of water for 10 minutes. Drink this three times daily. If you are using this herb in capsule form, the general dosage is three to nine grams per day.

Valerian

Valerian is a very calming herb that can help to alleviate anxiety, nervousness, muscle tension and insomnia, all of which are common symptoms of depression. Since this herb does have a sedative effect, it is usually taken before bed each day. The general dosage is 400 to 900 milligrams per day.

Lavender

Lavender is a very calming herb that helps to alleviate depression. It also has a positive impact on a variety of depression symptoms, such as added stress, headaches, tension and insomnia. This herb is most commonly used in essential oil form, but there are oral supplements that you can consider. When you are looking for a supplement, look for one that has 25 to 46 percent linalool. Once you find one, the general dose is 80 to 160 milligrams per day. Some people take a single dose before bed to promote sleep, but the dosage can be broken up to two to three times daily.

Passion Flower

Passion flower is commonly used to treat depression symptoms like anxiousness, agitation, restlessness, tension and insomnia. It helps to calm the body and mind, making it easier for you to relax. It helps to relax your mind by boosting GABA levels in the brain so that your brain activity is able to slow down. Several studies show that passion flower helps to promote better sleep when taken shortly before going to bed. It also works to reduce anxiety and stress, especially in those whose stress and anxiety are related to other conditions, such as depression.

You can use passion flower in both tea and oral capsule form. To make a tea, take a cup of boiling water and add a tablespoon of dry passion flower leaves. You should steep this mixture for 15 minutes. You can drink this three times a day. If you choose to take the capsule form of this herb, the average dose is 90 milligrams of passion flower per day. This dose is generally taken before you go to bed as a sleep aid.

Chapter 7.
Challenge Negative Thoughts

Negative thinking is something that everyone does from time to time, however, those suffering from depression are at risk for being controlled by it. It influences your decisions and has a major impact on your mood. When you fall into negative thinking, it also makes it a lot harder to fight your depression, so it is important to get this type of thinking under control.

The first step is identifying your negative thoughts so that you can work to counter them and turn them into something positive. When you start to feel emotions like anger, frustration, irritability, depressed mood or anxiousness, take a minute to think about why you feel this way. This gives you a minute to reflect on what is happening and what is causing these emotions. You want to do four things what you are experiencing negative emotions to identify your negative thoughts and overcome them:

Test Reality

Test the reality of your negative thoughts by asking yourself the following:

- What evidence supports my current thinking?

- Am I jumping to a negative conclusion?

- Are my thoughts interpretations or are they factual?

- How can I determine if these thoughts are true?

Seek Alternative Explanations

Ask yourself these questions to see if there are alternative explanations:

- What could this mean?

- What other ways can I explore this situation?

- How would I see this situation if I were being positive?

Put it in Perspective

Put your thinking and feelings in perspective by asking yourself these questions:

- Is this situation really as bad as I see it?

- What great things can happen in this situation?

- What is good about this situation?

- Will this situation even matter in five years?

- How likely is something bad to happen and what is the worst that can happen?

- What is likely to happen?

Utilize Goal-Directed Thinking

Ask yourself the following questions to take advantage of goal-directed thinking:

- Are my thoughts helping me to reach my goals?

- Can I learn something from this situation?

- What can I do to solve the problem?

These four steps allow you to work through your negative thoughts so that you can explore their origin so that you can prevent them in the future. When you recognize negative thoughts and take the time to address them, you are working toward thinking more positively naturally. This means that you will be less likely to experience negative thoughts in the future. You will gain a new perspective and be able to use it effectively to transform your thoughts into something that helps you to move forward.

There are four other things that you can do to work toward challenging your negative thoughts and feelings. Consider the following methods for helping you to think more positively:

- **Talk it out:** Find someone who you trust who knows you well and talk about your negative thoughts and feelings. The key to talking about it with someone else is to get a fresh perspective to help you understand, recognize and undo your negative thinking.

- **Get relaxed:** Take a few minutes each day and do something relaxing that allows you to get inside your own head and consider your thoughts. Things like meditation and yoga are popular options because they help you to open your mind so that you can focus on the thoughts that you are having.

- **Improve your physical health:** When you are working on your physical health, this often boosts your confidence. Those with more confidence tend to naturally think more positively. This also gives you positive things in your life to focus on.

- **Write it down:** When you are having negative thoughts, take a minute to write them down. You can look at them later in the day to determine where your negative thoughts were coming from. This will allow you to make the changes necessary to become a more positive person. It also helps you to identify that factors that cause you to have negative thoughts.

Chapter 8. Mind-Body Techniques

Mind-body techniques work on the idea that physical health is influenced by emotional factors. This means that you need to improve both physical and emotional health to have optimal total health. These techniques help you to balance your emotions so that you enjoy great health. There are a variety of mind-body techniques that can be helpful for depression, including:

Biofeedback

Biofeedback allows you to learn how to control your involuntary body practices, such as your heart rate. You use a monitor to see if your efforts are working. With depression, you can use biofeedback to reduce things like muscle tension and headaches.

Meditation

Meditation allows you to better focus your thoughts. When you meditate, you work to release your negative emotions by confronting them and working on ways to make them something positive. There are two primary types of meditation that you can practice, including:

- **Mindfulness meditation:** This type involves learning to focus on the moment and current sensations.

- **Transcendental meditation:** This type involves repeating a mantra.

Relaxing Physical Activity

There are two main types of physical activity that are also relaxing and promote a greater level of focus and concentration and these include tai chi and yoga. Tai chi is a type of martial arts that includes deep breathing and fluid movements.

Yoga involves fluid movements and working to center yourself. Both of these promote a sense of inner calm to improve your mood.

Acupuncture

Acupuncture is an ancient technique in which a qualified practitioner uses very fine needles and places them into specific points on the body. This Traditional Chinese Medicine technique is used for a wide array of health ailments, including depression. After your acupuncture session, the energy flow in your body is back inbalance, resulting in a boosted mood and a reduction in other depression symptoms.

Your acupuncturist may simply insert the needles and allow you to relax for 10 to 20 minutes and this is it. However, they may also manipulate the needles, depending on the technique used. When they manipulate the needles, they may gently twirl or move them, apply mild electrical pulses or apply mild heat.

Massage

Massage has over two dozen health benefits and one of these is helping to ease depression. This technique is beneficial for depression because it increases dopamine and serotonin and reduces cortisol levels. Both dopamine and serotonin are brain chemicals known as neurotransmitters. Both of these chemicals play a critical role in stabilizing the mood.

Cortisol is a hormone that can make stress and the related issues worse. When you get a massage, this can reduce cortisol levels by up to 50 percent. This works to alleviate your stress and depression symptoms.

Guided Imagery

Guided imagery is a mind-body technique that works to create harmony between your body and mind. You use all of your senses to focus your imagination to create a mental escape from depression and your symptoms. This is a powerful natural technique that improves your coping skills and gives you an outlet to deal with your depression in a positive and constructive way.

Chapter 9. Music and Art Therapy

Both music therapy and art therapy are proven to reduce depression and its symptoms. Both of these are a type of expressive therapy which helps you to express your thoughts and emotions via creativity. Many people with depression find it difficult to accurately verbalize what they are experiencing, but they are able to do this via music and art. Music and art give you an alternative way to convey and communicate your emotions and thoughts.

There are many ways for you to take advantage of music therapy, including:

- Creating music

- Singing songs that you create or songs that promote a positive mood

- Listening to music that makes you happy and boosts your mood

- Dancing to music that makes you feel happy and positive

Music therapy for depression is becoming more mainstream because it is a treatment that can work for everyone. It is highly adjustable so that everyone can find a way to use it to promote a better mood and a reduction in depression symptoms.

You can start using music therapy at home by simply using music as a way to express your thoughts and emotions. You may want to write song lyrics that describe how you feel or listen to music that counteracts a negative mood. Many people also find dancing to music beneficial because dancing is a form of physical activity. Physical activity causes a release of endorphins, a type of brain chemical that gives you an instant mood boost. In fact, dancing for 10 minutes to songs that make you happy can give you a quick mood boost when you are feeling down.

Art therapy is another option that you can use to fight depression. Common types of art used in art therapy include:

- Drawing or sketching

- Working with clay and ceramics

- Painting

- Making crafts

- Art journaling

- Mixed media art

You can also use certain exercises to help express your feelings through art. The first exercise involves closing your eyes and just scribbling. Make sure that the paper that you use does not move by taping it to the table. Use a crayon or a piece of chalk so that it flows easily. Now, close your eyes and just scribble for about 30 seconds. Examine your picture and title it.

Keep a journal that you can draw in to replace a writing journal. It works like a writing journal, but you just draw your thoughts and feelings instead. You can also use it for mixed media art or art journaling. The key is that you use this journal as a way to express your thoughts and feelings when you have difficulty verbalizing them.

Everyone has images that help them to feel calm and relaxed. You can create an image book with these images so that you can browse it when you are feeling especially down and depressed. Make sure that the images that you choose are positive and work to help you feel calm and happy. You can cut pictures from magazines, add photos of people you love and even add some drawings.

You can use both art therapy and music therapy to fight depression. People who use both forms of therapy tend to experience a greater reduction in their depression symptoms. Both of these techniques are easy to adjust to what works for you. Both also work to give you a release so that you are not allowing your negative emotions to accumulate and worsen your depression symptoms.

Chapter 10.
Aromatherapy

Aromatherapy is an ancient healing technique that utilizes essential oils to positively improve a person's mental state. Essential oils come from a variety of plant parts, such as the seeds, blossoms, roots and leaves. Practitioners blend the parts together to create a scent that possesses healing powers. There are many ways to use aromatherapy for depression and research shows that this natural technique does help to reduce the symptoms of depression to boost a person's mood.

Exactly how this technique works remains unknown, but scientists believe that the natural essential oil chemicals trigger the nose's cell receptors which are connected to certain areas of the brain. These areas are associated with your mood, so when you smell an essential oil, your mood improves and you feel a sense of calm. There are two main theories to explain how aromatherapy improves depression.

Strong aromas are known to influence the brain's limbic system. The brain reacts positively when you smell certain scents. For example, you experience relaxation and calmness when you smell lavender. The other theory lies behind a pharmacological effect. This means that certain essential oils work like antidepressants without the potential for side effects.

There are many ways to use aromatherapy and these are simple and convenient:

- **Room spray:** You can create a room spray by mixing essential oils with water and putting this into a spray bottle. Simply spray this mixture in the room that you are in to reap the benefits of the essential oils that you use.

- **Baths:** You can add several types of essential oils to your bath water and relax while getting the benefits of essential oils.

- **Diffusion:** There are aromatherapy diffusers that work to slowly release the scent of essential oils throughout a room in your home. This is a very common way to use essential oils because it allows for the highest level of control and a continuous release of the oils.

- **Massage:** After mixing essential oils with the right carrier oils, they can be used as a type of therapeutic massage oil. If you go for a massage, you can request which oils are used to ensure relief from your depression symptoms.

- **Body care products:** Take an unscented lotion, or other type of body care product, and add your favorite anti-depressant essential oils. Make sure to also add the right carrier oils. This allows you to constantly have the scent around you all throughout the day.

- **Steam:** You can boil water on the stove, add a few drops of essential oils and the scent will spread throughout the room

- **Dry evaporation:** Take essential oils that work to boost the mood and apply them to clean cotton balls. Take the cotton balls and place them close to you to continuously benefit from the scent.

The only thing to be aware of when using essential oils is that if you are allergic to a plant or herb, you will also be allergic to the associated essential oil. Because of this, if you have allergies, simply avoid the herbs associated with your known allergens. You also need to ensure that you use carrier oils when you use aromatherapy topically to avoid skin irritation. Other than these two precautions, aromatherapy is very safe.

When you are using essential oils for any topical application, you need a carrier oil to allow for proper dilution. In general, you will take a teaspoon of your chosen carrier oil and add three drops of your chosen essential oil to it. However, some oils require more dilution so make sure to read the bottle's label for adequate dilution. The following are common carrier oils that also benefit the skin:

- Grapeseed oil

- Apricot kernel oil

- Sweet almond oil

- Avocado oil

- Jojoba oil

None of the carrier oils will affect the scent of the essential oils. Make sure to refrigerate your carrier oils to prevent them from getting rancid.

You can use essential oils separately or create a mixture to reduce the symptoms of depression. Multiple single oils will be discussed in this chapter, but first, there is a common essential oil mixture that is well-known for being uplifting. Combine the following to create a powerful uplifting aromatherapy mixture:

- Six drops of bergamot oil

- Three drops of geranium oil

- Three drops of petitgrain oil

- One drop of neroli oil

- Two ounces of your chosen carrier oil

Once you mix this together, you can use it in the way that you prefer. Make a room spray, add it to unscented body lotion, place it on a cotton ball or add it to your diffuser. It is best to make it exactly per the recipe and do not add anything extra. This ensures the most benefit from this aromatherapy combination.

The following essential oils can be used together or individually to boost your mood and alleviate the symptoms of depression:

- **Bergamot:** This essential oil is very refreshing and it helps to give you a boost of energy. It reduces depression-related pain, anxiety and sadness, and helps to uplift your spirit.

- **Clary sage:** This scent is very popular for inducing sleep when you are experiencing insomnia. It also helps with depression and anxiety symptoms.

- **Geranium:** This oil helps you to release negative emotions. It lifts your spirits, acts as a natural sedative and reduces stress.

- **Lemon:** Lemon is a very uplifting and purifying scent with refreshing properties. Other benefits include reducing stress, combatting negative emotions and boosting your immune system.

- **Mandarin:** Mandarin uplifts your spirit to cause a better mood. It can also reduce muscle tension associated with depression because it works as an antispasmodic.

- **Wild orange:** Like the other citrus essential oils, this scent is energizing, refreshing and it has the ability to lift your mood. It also helps to reduce feelings of anger, nervousness, panic and irritation.

- **Rose:** Rose helps to induce a significant sense of overall well-being. It also stimulates the nervous system to boost your energy.

- **Sandalwood:** Sandalwood is a very popular essential oil that helps to fight inner stress and ease tension. These benefits are due to it having sedative properties and the ability to comfort you.

- **Basil:** Basil works well to fight against the symptoms of fatigue, anxiety and depression. It is also refreshing and uplifting.

- **Frankincense:** This essential oil is one of the oldest ones. It helps to reduce feelings of nervous tension, anxiety, fear and stress because it helps you to slow your breathing so that you are able to better focus and relax.

- **Jasmine:** Jasmine is a floral scent that induces relaxation and uplifts you. It can also relieve depression-related tension due to its antispasmodic properties.

- **Lavender:** Lavender is one of the most popular essential oils for depression and it is truly a cure-all type of oil. For depression, it helps to relax and calm the mind and body. It is also beneficial for headaches, fear, nervousness, insomnia, migraines, anxiety and high blood pressure.

- **Marjoram:** This essential oil is commonly used to ease feelings of loneliness, rejection, fear, grief and anxiety.

- **Palmarosa:** This scent is common for reducing anxiety and nervous tension. This allows you to relax and get comfortable. These effects also work to reduce the risk of insomnia.

- **Roman chamomile:** Next to lavender, this is probably the most common essential oil for depression. The scent helps to relax and calm your mind and body. It is very commonly used as a natural treatment for stress and depression.

- **Ylang-ylang:** This oil works to balance female and male energies due to its ability to deeply relax you. This scent is popular for anxiety, depression and insomnia. It also helps to restore both equilibrium and confidence.

- **Tangerine:** This scent is very interesting because it has the ability to increase your energy while also being sedating at the same time. This allows for you to feel simultaneously awake and alert, but also calm.

- **Osmanthus:** This essential oil is most common in Traditional Chinese Medicine. It is uplifting and sweet.

- **Elemi:** This is not a very common essential oil, but it works well to calm your nervous system. It also aids in alleviating stress.

- **Birch:** This essential oil does not work to alleviate depression directly, but a common symptom. Those with depression commonly experience muscle stiffness and pain and this oil works to alleviate these.

- **Cinnamon:** Cinnamon is a popular spice, but it can also help with the symptoms of depression when used in aromatherapy. It helps to prevent sleepiness so that you have more energy, and it decreases irritability.

- **Neroli:** Neroli is a very comforting essential oil. It helps to relieve depression at its core and improve emotional exhaustion.

- **Grapefruit:** This scent is very uplifting. It helps to boost your mood and increase energy.

- **Orange:** Orange essential oil improves your energy and your mood.

There are many different blends that you can use when you want to reduce several symptoms of depression at once. Consider the following four blends to get started with aromatherapy for depression:

Blend Number One

- One drop of rose oil

- One drop of orange oil

- Three drops of sandalwood oil

Blend Number Two

- Two drops of clary sage oil

- Three drops of bergamot oil

Blend Number Three

- One drop of ylang-ylang oil

- One drop of lavender oil

- Three drops of grapefruit oil

Blend Number Four

- One drop of lemon oil

- Two drops of frankincense oil

- Two drops of neroli

- Two drops of jasmine

Conclusion

Depression has a significant impact on all aspects of your life. As soon as symptoms begin, it is important that you start taking the steps to treat this illness. You now have the tools that you need to treat your depression naturally. Use a combination of these methods to ensure that you get to the root cause of your depression while also alleviating your symptoms.

As you work through this book, start with one of the natural treatments for depression and concentrate on this before adding another one. This will help you to treat your depression without feeling overwhelmed with the process. It also helps you to gradually treat your illness.

This is important because abrupt changes in your life can actually worsen your depression.

The natural treatments for depression not only treat your depression, but they also help to improve your overall health. This makes a big difference because having additional health issues can actually feed into and worsen depression. When you work toward improving your overall health, you are simultaneously working to improve your mental and emotional health.

All of the natural treatments that are discussed in this guide are safe, but as always, make sure that you talk to your physician before starting with any new exercise regime, supplements or herbs. If you take any medications or have any other health conditions, you want to make sure that there will be no negative interactions. The whole purpose of treating your depression naturally is to recover without any negative effects and talking to your doctor first can help to ensure this.

Once you recover from depression, use this book as a preventative measure so that you do not relapse. Using these treatments and remedies are equally beneficial as preventative strategies for depression. These all help you to keep your mood elevated and alleviate the stress and worries that contribute to depression.

It is most important to remember that there is hope and you can recover from depression. While this condition can be serious, it is very treatable. You can also prevent a relapse. Use the strategies in this book to help improve all aspects of your health and start enjoying a life that is happy, whole and fulfilled.